Inspirations

Poetry and Artwork

By

Rosemarie McCoy

Inspirations

Poetry and Artwork

By

Rosemarie McCoy

*Copyright © 1994 by
the children of Rosemarie McCoy*

ISBN: 0-9641925-0-0

*Library of Congress
Catalog Card Number: 94-96249*

*Prepared and Arranged for Publication
by the children of Rosemarie McCoy*

*All rights reserved.
No part of this publication may be reproduced or transmitted in
any form by any means, electronic or mechanical, including
photocopy, recording, or any information storage or retrieval
system, without written permission from the
children of Rosemarie McCoy.*

Printed in United States of America

PINE HILL PRESS, INC.
Freeman, S. Dak. 57029

About the Author

Rosemarie Huls was born in 1929 and grew up on a farm near Montrose, South Dakota. She attended elementary school at Salem St. Mary's and graduated from Humboldt High School. She attended General Beadle State Teachers College and taught in a country school for a few years.

In 1949, she married Celestine "Mac" McCoy. She devoted her life to raising her six daughters and two sons.

She was an Avon representative for 17 years. She enjoyed writing, gardening, bowling, swimming and painting.

Rosemarie died on April 11, 1992. Her husband preceded her in death on February 25, 1990.

In Memory of Rosemarie McCoy

This book is dedicated to our mother, Rosemarie McCoy, for her love and devotion to her family. Mother has written poetry since we were young children and always had a dream of publishing her poems. As a family we have gathered her collection in a way in which we hope she would have.

We will always Love You Mom! xxxooxxxoooxxxooo

*****

I am proud to say that Rosemarie McCoy was my first cousin. Rose was a lady always ready to capture the given moment. Her spiritual zeal.....her cherished family ties.....her patriotic spirit.....her love and appreciation for nature were always evident.

This collection of poems typifies the yearning Rose had to preserve the celebration of life each day. No event ever seemed to be over when it was over. Through her marvelous gift of writing and her love for writing, you will see that Rose would capture the moment and continue to cherish it on paper.

The printing of these poems serves as a special tribute to Rose and will continue to preserve her desire to capture the moment and allow one to relive the moment.....that wonderful historic event of family and community.....those expressions depicting marvelous gifts of nature.

Father Bob Krantz

Poetry Chapters

Inspirations In Faith

Family

Love

Life

Nature

Friendship

Patriotism

Searching For Strength

Poetry by Celestine (Mac) McCoy

Inspirations In Faith

Inspirations

*If I am to express myself in poetry and love
Let my words flow from up above,
Let my poems do some good
Let the words say what they should,
Let my thoughts be good and pure
Keep these inspirations ever near;
If you are miserable and very blue
Let there be a poem just for you,
Let the words cheer your unhappy heart
And brighten your day from the very start,
If you are happy and very gay
Spread your happiness with your smiles today,
If you are retarded and cannot express your thought,
If you are handicapped and cannot walk,
If you are blest with sight but cannot talk,
If you can hear but cannot see,
You will be blest eternally;
There is One that loves us all
He will help us stand straight and tall,
With His help my poems will progress
And there will be one that will bring you happiness,
For happiness comes in many ways
In the little things we do today,
Put yourself in the trust of Him
Who guides us all with our conscience from within,
If I am to express myself in poetry and love
Let my poems be inspired from Him above.*

Let Me Key Your Mind To Mine

Read carefully and hear what I say,
Think my thoughts as you read today
I want you to feel as I have felt
And see the things I have seen,
I want you to travel the places I have been
And dream the dreams I dream,
Walk with me when I walk
Run with me when I run, skip with me and fly,
I will stir your imagination,
And draw for you a magic pattern in the sky,
AND I WILL TRY!
To give you a glimpse of heaven
While during your stay on earth,
As we travel o'er America
The heritage of our birth.

Creation

God gave us the moon, the stars,
        the sun, the flowers,
To love and enjoy,
        these treasures are ours.

With Us He Will Stay

*God appeared in the sky today
In the form of sun
Then faded away,
He comes to us in many ways
If we have faith
With us He'll stay.*

Heaven's Answering Service

*I have a moral issue to decide,
What will be my answer, who will be my guide?
The Ten Commandments, is a good place to start,
Then there is my conscience, what say my heart?
I could ask my parents or counselors to advise,
But I think I will ask God, that would be wise.*

Serenity

To know serenity one must awaken
While the rest of the world sleeps,
That moment when the world is quiet
And at peace with itself;
A moment when the world stands still
And even the birds are not restless;
When the only movement is that of the leaves
Swaying in the gentle breeze;
The only light is God's light
From His universe, His home.
He knows serenity and has made His peace our peace;
His world, our world;
Oh God, chase away inner torments.
Let everyone know peace within himself
And know serenity;
As I know serenity at this moment.

Farewell 'Til Tomorrow

*Have you seen a tree with one little leaf,
One little leaf, tattered and torn,
Poor little leaf, wind-swept and worn?
Bid your good-byes, next year it will be reborn.
As a leaf I too shall leave you
For I am growing withered and worn,
I too have lived through many a storm,
Soon I will know the breath of a new morn,
Together we will be reborn.*

Today's Prayer For The Future

*Our future belongs to our children
And the careers they have sought,
Soon we will be too old
To do the things we were taught.*

*May the blessing of Your presence, Lord
Accompany those chosen careers,
Help them to build a world of better people
As they venture through the years.*

Untitled

*A child at play —
Caused me to smile today.
It erased the loneliness I felt —
Then I knelt to pray.*

Little Lost Girl

*Have you ever seen the blackness
Of the very blackest night?
Have you ever looked about you
And saw no starry light?
You feel so terribly lonely
On the loneliest of nights.
As the darkness shrouds around you,
"Have Faith";
You are not alone, God is in sight!*

Untitled

*A little child walked into the church one day
And up the middle aisle he walked.
He knelt down at the communion rail
To the Crucifix he talked.
Say do You love me God?
My mother says You do.
Well then how much do You love me,
If what she says is true?
Do You love me more than a penny's worth?
Or more than a dollar can buy?
Or could it be a hundred dollar's worth?
I guess that is going too high.
The little child listened then
He wanted to hear God's voice.*

*And God just had to answer,
He had no other choice.
Oh! yes My child, I love you
And more than all the world's great wealth
Is the love I have for you.
And you know I would like to reach down My hand to you
And clasp you up to Me.
But I can't
Because of love for you,
They are pinned to a cross-shaped tree.
So never forget that I love you My child
And may I ask one thing of you
Because I have loved you
Won't you try to love Me too?*

A Prayer For Help

O Heavenly Father
Teach me to pray,
Make me a better parent
As I go through the day.

Help me teach my children
To be honest and kind,
That honesty brings happiness
And keeps healthy their minds.

Let me praise the children
For their good today,
Keep me from degrading them
In what I say.

Let me be courteous
Help me to understand,
Keep me from being unreasonable
By making too many demands.

Make me patient
Teach me to pray,
And if I need Your help
Let me turn to You today.

*Let my punishments
Be right and just,
Help the children to love me
And in me place their trust.*

*Bless me with bigness
To grant reasonable requests,
Let me be friendly
To their guests.*

*Let them make their own decisions
And if they are wrong,
Help me to say no
Let me be strong.*

*My children are children
Teach me not to expect,
The judgment of adults
Give me their respect.*

*All this I want
As I pray today,
O Heavenly Father
Please hear what I say.*

Help Me Enter Port

I am all Yours Lord
Help me enter port.
My ship was set-a-sailing
Faltering on the sea,
It was small and helpless
And needed help from Thee.

My sails were bright and shining
Kept clean by rain and sun,
My little ship kept sailing
With Your help, Thy will be done.

I felt You in the misty breeze
As I floundered in the sea,
I knew I had to stop and pray
And get some help from Thee.

My ship kept sailing slower
Many directions it did take,
My vessel filled with right and wrong
I thought my hull would break.

I cannot let my vessel sink
Because of lack of care,
I must take the time to think
And put my ship in good repair.

I will drop my heavy anchor
Along Your sandy shore,
I'll stop to chip my barnacles off
Your help I do implore.

Now that I have cleansed my ship
May my faith increase,
For I want to sail to heaven
A place of lasting peace.

Family

Mother

*Have you ever thought of every word
That you have ever known?
And as the words slipped through your tongue
Only one has shown of gold.
Yes, this precious word is Mother.*

*I've looked through my dictionary
To find the meaning that is true,
But the only one that was really right
Is the one described by you.
Yes, this precious person is Mother.*

*Mother could mean beautiful, wonderful, and kind,
You could describe her as intelligent, generous, and strong;
Any word that you could use,
Could never be counted wrong.
Yes, these precious words mean Mother.*

*Yes, I think she is all of these,
And many, many more,
My one wish to fulfill my life, is she knows my thoughts,
Before she passes through heaven's own door.
Yes, this Precious Person is Mother.*

Remember Mother on her special day!

These Are The Bonds

There is no bond like the family bond,
That binds us all together.

The sounds of laughter and the sounds of fun,
The sounds of glee from the little one,
The sounds of cries and the sight of tears,
The parents love that calms the fears,
These are the bonds.

The gurgle and burp and the baby's first cry,
The beautiful smile as he waves good-bye,
When they learn to crawl and they begin to walk,
They mimic and murmur as they learn to talk,
These are the bonds.

The sight of the little ones on their trikes,
The sight of the older ones on their bikes,
The sound of the ball that hits the bat,
The purring sound of the family cat,
These are the bonds.

Bumps on the head and bruises on the knees,
Do's and don'ts, and will you say please?
Sharing and not sharing as they learn to play,
The fun versus hardships that make up the day,
These are the bonds.

The pat by the father on the little child's head,
Hugs and kisses as they prepare for bed,
The sound of the footsteps on the stairs,
The fold of their hands as they say their prayers,
These are the bonds.

The trials and errors as we go through life,
The days and nights that are filled with strife,
Sense of accomplishment for work well done,
The treasures we reap with the setting sun,
These are the bonds that bind us all together.

Golden Years

Many years have passed since that wondrous day
Blest with sunshine and hopeful rays,
When at St. Agatha's you made your vows
To love, to cherish, never to part,
And together you felt peace within your hearts.
Just as farming was part of your life,
So is the happiness and sadness you knew as man and wife.
Fourteen children were born to you
A living proof of love so true,
You spent many hours molding clay
We have you to thank for what we are today.
With your guidance, courage, and perseverance, we grew strong.
You taught us to know right from wrong.
Thanks Mother and Dad for precious memories
Of times we spent with you,
Those growing-up years, interludes of tears, and happiness too.
To know you is to love you.
God has given you fifty years together.
Young years, tender years, loving years,
Golden years together.
God Bless You.

For You The Bell Rings

I heard the bell ring in a special way
Atop St. Joseph's on Mother's Day,
It rang for you mother, mother my love,
A message to you from the angels above,
For I spoke to them in my prayers last night
And asked them if with the morning light,
They would sing to Our Lady, Our Mother above,
For she is Our Lady, "Our Lady of Love,"
And she with her tenderness would impart
Words that are buried within my heart,
And a message would ring throughout the land
To say to the world, here is a lady grand,
One who sacrificed and dedicated her life
Being a good mother and loving wife,
And "Our Lady," would reach out, reach out her hand,
To touch the loveliness of each graying strand,
And the bells would ring out, sing out to say,
"Have a Happy Mother's Day."

In honor of my mother, Agnes Huls,
on Mother's Day, 1969.

Father

O Heavenly Father
Hear our prayer,
Bless our father
For whom we care.

Bless him with good health
Let his smile be bright,
Let him know happiness
From morn to night.

O Heavenly Father
Hear our prayer,
Bless our father
For whom we care.

Please Help Mother Is My Prayer

I heard the bells, I heard them today,
They chimed in the chapel as I knelt to pray,
I looked for You God, I knew You were there
Help my mother, "Oh! Help!" is my prayer.
No one but You can keep her from pain
Please make her comfortable and happy again,
Take her soul and keep her for us,
For You are my God, in Whom I trust.

I Will Always Hear The Bells

The bells are ringing, ringing today
But now in the heavens far away,
Mother has gone to heaven above
To be with Our Lady, "Our Lady of Love,"
For Our Lady reached out, reached out her hand
And took mother with her to a distant land,
Far beyond space to wait for us
This I know, for God I trust.

Please Help My Father

My father needs you, needs you today
He is worried and sad with mother away,
He needs you desperately, please help him I pray,
And Blessed Mother I know, I feel you are here,
Please touch dad's shoulder and keep him from fear,
For 51 years they are married today
What more can I say, what more can I pray?
Please help.

Dearest On Father's Day

Now to get words that rhyme. I'll start,
You've now been a Father six times.
"Plenty I'd say, gives Pop something to be proud of today."

There's Cheryl, she is ten.
A sweeter more helpful girl, there could have never been.

Richard follows next in line, he's a boy you can be proud of any ol' time.

Vikki—your pixie, is close to your heart. With her sweet ways you never could part.

Nancy Jo, four, with golden locks to adore—she's bouncy and full of energy plus. With her bright sayings and happy smile, she'll see you through many an unhappy mile.

Loran James, your second boy, with his sparkling brown eyes is quite a joy. He loves to spend his time with you. His love for you—you can be sure is true.

Carolyn Jean, is our little dream. With you she shares this special day as she is going to be baptized this afternoon.

A tribute from Mother, comes straight from her heart,
I love you, I love you, I love you, Dear Heart.

Love from Mother and All

Cel

*I have so many goals to reach
And you are always there to encourage me,
And to praise me for little things.
But best of all
You are the Father of my children.*

*I shed a tear of happiness,
I know that I am loved.
Not because of the things I want to be,
But for the things I am.*

*You have never asked me to be perfect
You liked me as I am,
I couldn't ask for more.*

*Thanks for calling me "Your Girl"
For that is all I want to be.*

                    Love you Cel

Rose

Remember Me With Love

September of 1966

Dearest One,

It pains me to remember the times I have hurt you
It saddens me to think of the things I have said,
Why were some of the words so thoughtless?
When I would rather have said, "I Love You," instead.
So please forgive me for the wrong,
Let only the good invade your heart like a song.
Remember me with Love.

Forever, with love.

Lucky Pop On Fathers' Day

"May God Bless You," on this very special day,
And wipe all your worries and cares away;
We all love you more than words can say,
So love and kisses from your loved ones today.

You're a "Lucky Man," with a lovely wife,
With eight sweet kids, what a life!!!!
You're a lucky man and you know it,
So come on Pop, it's time to show it!

Sculptured By Two

Did you take your piece of modeling clay
And work with it with love today?
Did you straighten its spine with a kind word,
Did a smile appear because of what it heard?
Did it stride forth with a confident step
Because of a promise that you kept?
Is it singing a song and whistling a tune?
Then you have done well, but your job is not done,
Your work goes on from sun to sun.
For this clay that was given you
Is your son and your daughter
They need to be sculptured by two.

Whatever I Do

*Whatever I do
I wish to do well,
This means more to me
Than words can tell.*

*Not just a Wife
But a companion so true,
Able to express my love
In whatever I do.*

*Not just a Mother
But an understanding friend,
To set a good example
From beginning to end.*

*Not just a Cook
But one of a special kind,
A well balanced diet
To keep healthy bodies and minds.*

*Not just a Chauffeur
But a safe, thoughtful one,
A defensive driver who will see
The dangers that bring sorrow
To you and to me.*

*Not just a Housekeeper
But one who can spend
Her energies cleaning,
And save time to be wife,
Mother and friend.*

*Not just a Homemaker
But one who can share,
In civic activities
And social affairs.*

*I want to be a special Homemaker
So humble, generous, and true,
As this is the vocation
I have chosen to do.*

*Whatever I do
I wish to do well,
This means more to me
Than words can tell.*

Precious Moments

I get time with my child I would otherwise miss,
When she awakens in the middle of the night like this,
All she needs is T.L.C.
And this is what she gets from me.

T.L.C. tender loving care

Place For Baby

There is a place
Right in my arms,
For a snuggly baby
With all of its charms.

Thought Complete

Every poem I ever write about our children
I never complete without the thought,
That they are a gift from God;
They are only borrowed to us to love and enjoy,
Their future belongs to God and they will return to Him.

First Born

I paged today through my picture book
It brought a smile and yet a tear,
It started with your babyhood days
And ended today, this year;
You're now a grown young lady
An image of our love,
You're all we ever dreamed you would be
Our first born, Our gift from above.

To our oldest daughter Cheryl Marie

Happy Birthday To Our Daughter

Happy Birthday Daughter,
    You are 15 years today;
May the days that pass so quickly by,
    Be happy ones, we pray.

              Love from Mother and Dad

To our daughter Cheryl

A Rainy Day

*Confused paper boy,
First trip,
Running water
Papers drip,
No wire cutters
Forgot,
Never got started,
Before rain stopped.*

To my son Richard

You

*Your kindness to others
   is a quality blest.
Your helpfulness, your sweetness,
   your saucy manner too,
Make up you, you Vikki,
   the person we love.*

To our daughter Vikki

My Son

I look out the window
That's my boy,
I look out the window
My heart surges with joy,
He's clean-cut and wonderful
So straight and so small,
He's blond and he's handsome
As little boys are,
A gift from heaven
A gift from afar.

Written to my little son Loran James,
five years old.

Through The Eyes Of A Child

A color on the living room wall
A color I was not sure of at all,
A mixed color of beige and green
The strangest color I have ever seen,
I wasn't sure if I would like it
Until I heard a little boy's voice
As he worked beside his dad,
"This sure is a pretty color."
I now see what he sees
And now I am glad.

Children can make everything right
if you love and enjoy them.
To my son, Loran James

Growth

*As time moves all too swiftly by
And childhood disappears,
May your character grow in strength
As you travel through the years.
And through all of your experiences
May there emerge a man,
One who can make decisions,
And able to take a stand,
Full of love and understanding
A leader in our land.*

*God be with you Larry,
We love you.*

Mom

Children

*Merry Christmas loved ones.
May your eyes glow with happiness,
May your hearts be filled with joy,
May you show compassion in the things you do.
This is what I want,
This is what I expect of you.*

Mother

Gift From Heaven

*Her hair is soft and beautiful,
The curls keep tumbling down;
They fall upon her shoulders,
And make her shining crown.*

*When she was only three years old,
She became very ill one day;
Father Beck visited the hospital,
And confirmed her right away.*

*I chose the name of Mary,
Joseph's loving spouse;
I knew they would protect her,
And return her to our house.*

*She was so very ill,
We kept a vigil by her side;
Without the help from Mary,
She surely would have died.*

*This loving girl is with us,
Her name is Carolyn Jean;
We will always be thankful to Mary,
For giving us this Queen.*

*Her hair so soft and beautiful,
Her eyes so very brown,
Her beauty resembles that of Mary,
With spun gold for her crown.*

*To Carolyn Jean Mary, during her illness
with spinal meningitis in August of 1965.*

Our Little Star

*Out by the bush
Stood our little girl,
So little and wonderful
With a breath of a curl.*

*She watched the many squirrels
As they scampered in play,
This precious girl
Is Sandra Kay.*

*She chased the little animals
And laughed with glee,
This little daughter
Belongs to you and to me.*

*Sandra is a baby
Just past the age of two,
She's tiny and beautiful
With big eyes of blue.*

*She's an angel from heaven
A gift from afar,
A precious little darling
Our little Star.*

To our little daughter, Sandra Kay

A Little Mixed Up

Walk with me Mommy to kindergarten today.
"I want to go too," said three year old, Sandra Kay.
Then I took the children's hands,
And Sandy became our guide
She patrolled the corners and stopped us from walking,
Instead of STOP! LOOK!   and LISTEN!
She said, "LOOK! STOP   TALKING!"

Happy Birthday Sandy!

Dearest Sandy,
Time is passing too quickly
And someday soon
Dad and I will be standing alone . . .
In an empty room.
We'll feel your loss
Even though you've grown,
And gone on your way.
Beautiful memories,
We'll always have.
They are ours . . .
No one can take them away . . .

So grow if you must,
But always leave us your love
As we give ours to you.
And remember Home is where we are,
Love is where we are.
We'll always be here for you . . . . . .

              Mom

Sing Of Lisa

*I have a little baby
Her name is Lisa Rae,
I have a little baby
She takes a nap each day,
I have a little baby
Her lips are soft and round,
I have a little baby
With eyes big and brown,
Sing of Lisa.*

Lisa

*Lisa is one year old today,
There are a few words
She has learned to say,
It is ma_____ma and daddy,
Cheri and Hi!
When someone leaves
She waves good-bye.
She combs at her hair
And tugs at her shoes,
She hasn't learned yet
Stockings come by twos.
She smacks her lips and smiles so bright,
She snuggles in your arms,
When it is time for good-night;
There is spunk and spirit in this little tyke,
When she wants her way, she can really fight.*

Girls

Sing of little girls
Sing of curls and happiness
Smiles, laughter, love, and beauty
This is girls, loving girls, our girls.

To our six daughters

On The Most Wanted List

I'm on the most wanted list
They have my number,
They all want Mother
And will accept no other.
Don't want daddy, sister or brother
Mommy, Mommy,
I want my Mother!
I guess I love this
But sometimes I'm pressed,
I have a large family
Or haven't you guessed?
Are you on the most wanted list
In your city?
If you are not,
What a pity.

Seasons Present A Bit Of Confusion

One thing about winter when it comes
Children have lots of fun,
What I can't seem to get charged up about
Is dressing them up, to go out.
When there are two under three, and four under six,
To find the right clothes you perform some tricks.
The snow pants fit, but the jackets are small
Will the six fit the four, or is she too tall?
Give it to the three she has grown this year,
We'll give hers to the two, she is a baby dear;
This leaves pants that fit them all
But jackets, O My! they've grown since fall,
To the store they will go tonight
I will order two jackets and two pairs of boots,
I'll stay home and not go out
Let dad find out what the world is about,
The truth of the matter is
Before all are dressed to go out,
The first out is ready to come in
Then you start all over again.

Treasure Chest

*There was a time when I would hear
Each child's playful noise,
I'd say to each and everyone
Run along, and don't forget your toys!*

*I'd wonder as I watched them
With each little downcast face,
Why didn't I help them pick them up
And put them in their place.*

*I hurt a little in my heart
And took some time to think,
Each child is God's loving gift
And without them my spirit would sink.*

*Now I look intently at each child
And watch each tiny face,
Instead of childish mischievousness
I see beauty in its place.*

*For childhood is a magic moment
That passes too quickly by,
I want to capture those wispy moments
And treasure them until I die.*

Mommy's Love Will Help You

*Are you afraid little darling
When you awaken at night,
Do all the sounds of darkness
Give you quite a fright?*

*Then mommy will buy you a flashlight
And when you hear a sound,
You can sit right up in your bed
And flash the light around.*

*Won't it be fun to see
That you are not alone,
That you have your warm little bed
That is your very own?*

*If you open your sleepy eyes
And you really look around,
Your teddy bear and dolly
Never heard a sound.*

*When you see that all is right
Brave little child shut off your light,
Then dream of angels
'Til the morn is light.*

Tribute To Emil

What a beautiful tribute,
The endless chain of love.
Family, Relatives, Friends
Embracing in the celebration
Of Emil's entrance into heaven.

May God be always with you,
His family, as you and all of us
Wait with Him for the time
When we are called.

Untitled

The church was filled with people
And our tears have overflowed.
We extend our hearts and hands
As our love for you unfolds.
May the love you shared in your lifetime,
And our love we extend to you
Give you courage and peace of mind.

Nettie

God bless you Aunt Nettie
In the name of the Father and
Of the Son and of the Holy Spirit.

We gather together
To bid good-bye
But we really know
You didn't die.

Your days are finished
Your nights are done
Your soul has risen
Like the morning sun.

You have gained heaven
With kindness and love
You have met your Lord
In the heavens above.

God has blest you.

Barney And Glady

Crazy kids
Yes you are
Age makes
No difference
Grab a star
Hang on for
Dear life
And enjoy
Time together
As man and wife

Grandmother's Thanks

I talked to my granddaughter about her home away from home and wondered what she would say. She said, "I have lots of fun and go there everyday."

"My brother goes there too," she said. "He is just a little boy. They wipe his nose and change his pants and he plays with lots of toys."

"When he falls they pick him up and kiss him where it hurts. They do the things that mommies do, they even change his shirt."

"I am bigger than my brother," she said, with a twinkle in her eye. "When I fall, I pick myself up, I even don't cry."

"You know they took us to the zoo. We ran and laughed and played. We fed the animals, watched the ducks, and stayed there most of the day."

"But there are other things to do that are not always fun. We have to pick our toys up when we are done. We have to be quiet and sleep, we can't always laugh and play. Even though we are happy, we are glad at the end of the day."

"Why is that?" I asked, and this is what she said, "Mommy and Daddy pick us up and hug us very tight, and we are really glad to go home with them every night. Then Grandma, you know what? The next day we do the same. Back to daycare, school and fun, and the teachers say, they are glad we came."

I smiled amused as grandmothers do, knowing the children get good care. Now I can rest and close my eyes and give thanks to God as I remember you in my prayers.

Dedicated to the teachers at the Children's Center, where my grandchildren Shanel and Anthony attended in 1991.

Ruby Wedding Anniversary
40 Years

I thought of this a little late
To bring this poem up-to-date,
I am no poet — as you can see
So come along and bear with me.

Some of the poem will be happy
Some humorous, some sad,
But it will prove that we are glad
To have known two as wonderful as Mom and Dad!

Now 15 more years have vanished
Yes, those 15 years have fled
Since their 25th Anniversary.
And 40 years have past since they were wed.

Forty long years together
With a love they shared with all,
Among the days that they'll remember
Happy times they will recall
May this anniversary be treasured
As nicest of them all.

To Montrose they moved from Salem
To start life anew — May God bless these two.

The land was hilly and rocky
And Dad put it to the test —
And through all his patience and toil,
Their crops were not the best.

*Here they met many new neighbors and friends
That were really warm and true,
It helped to keep them from remembering
How much they missed all of you.*

*As Dad was tilling the soil,
Mother was busy, the dear,
Getting ready for three weddings, all within one year.*

*First came Betty and Leo on February 6, 1945
It was a cold, cold stormy day,
This didn't stop them, they were married anyway.
Some humorous, did I say?*

*Just four months later, Marty and Margaret were wed.
It rained and rained that day,
This didn't stop them either, they were married that day.
But their happiness showed through the clouds
Like sunshine, on this all important day.*

*On January 8, 1946
There was another lovely bride and charming groom,
Dorothy and Emil said their life they would share
And congratulations went out to the happy pair.*

*Life then went back to its normal pace, until 1948
When Art and Margaret hurried to the altar
So they wouldn't be late.
May the happy turn of fortune
That brought them together —
Make their love grow even deeper
And guide them through all weather.*

*Then on one bleak December day
Our dear Vernon passed away.
This day we will all remember — but life must go on
Sadness kept us all together and made us strong.*

*While all this was happening — older I got,
And Cel put me on the spot!
"Marry me," he said,
So on September 20, 1949 we were wed.
I won't add anymore — ********
I'll go on with this poem instead.*

*Three more years went quickly by
We'll go to June the month of brides
When Marie and Ray spoke their vows
And again at St. Agatha's
Wedding bells rang clear and loud!
And here's to the happy man and wife
Sharing the joys of married life.*

*This family celebrates more than any I know
'Cause six days later to another wedding they go
Here's a knot that was really tied
As Vincent and Yvonne
Tried their wedding rings on for size!*

*Mom and Dad farmed in Montrose, eight years in one place
Another record few can trace.*

*To a farm near Sioux Falls they moved from there
Still the two steadfast pair.*

*Then in September of 1955
Lowell and LaWanda became man and wife
They've had almost four years experience
In glad married life.*

*After many fruitless years of farming
And no future could they see,
Dad took a look and without new equipment
He could never balance the books
So together they decided to sell.*

*As they watched their things being sold
Some new, some old
They shed a tear or two.
Our hearts went out to them that day,
When all they knew and loved
Was sold and trucked away.*

*They with Lyle, Ronald, Barbara, and Jerry
Have faced life anew,
And always there is sunshine
In the beautiful skies of blue.*

*Soon to their new home they will move,
A dream come true.*

*Love and friendship, dreams come true
Glad and long years for you!*

*Thank you for listening to my jabber
I am afraid I got carried away
Best wishes to Mom and Dad
On this, their Anniversary Day.*

Love

Untitled

*Think of one word
Is it love?
Is it joy?
Dwell upon this word
Let it enter your body
Surround your soul.*

*Maybe you are afraid
You will become strong.
Maybe you are sad
You will feel joy.
Maybe you are lonely
You will find a friend.
For God is love.*

Love

*Love is a whispered word, a silent prayer.
A touch. A tear.
A deep longing when you are not here.*

Melody Of Love

*Through the fragrant scent of springtime
With the warmth from the setting sun,
Shines the love of two people
Endearing to each other, in the sanction of one.*

A Phrase

"I love you," is a spontaneous phrase
That passes one's lips, that is true;
"I love you," is a precious phrase,
Delivered from me to you.

"I love you," is so enchanting
It passes your lips and mine;
This phrase is so spontaneous,
It is uttered anytime.

Love Is Happiness

Don't keep your love locked up inside
Let your heart be your guide,
All the wonderful words found in books
Can be said, can show in your looks,
Don't be timid, don't be proud
Speak your praises strong and loud,
Never hide your love, let it show
Life is too short to hide the glow,
Bring happiness while you can
Or someday you'll remember
"What might-have-been."

Song In Our Hearts

"I love you," is sung from the corners of the earth,
"I love you," has been sung since the day of birth,
It is sung by the young and sung by the old
Sung by the shy ones, the quiet, and bold,
It is sung from the North, the South, East, and West,
Sing it day, sing it night, anytime is best,
If there is love in your life you can meet any test,
So sing to the winds, "I love you."

Remember Him With Love

His kiss is wet against my cheek
I feel it lingering there,
It stayed with me throughout the day
I knew he really cared.

As your loved one kisses you
Do you say a prayer,
That there will always be a loving kiss
Waiting for you there?

Today Is Forever

Today is the Wedding
Gay and bright,
A wonderful beginning
Before candlelight.

Today you go forth
Hand in hand,
Two people as one
In this great land.

Keep your life glowing
Cherish and love,
A beautiful partnership
Joined by God above.

Let no man put asunder
This relationship gay,
Keep this beautiful beginning
As it is today.

Remember

Remember the day
Beautiful and bright,
Remember the altar
With its candlelight,
Remember how we pledged
Our love that night,
How we would never let the sun go down
Without making things right?
Maybe we have forgotten,
But it's not too late;
We have shared much in these 15 years
And you still rate,
So let's pledge anew
Our love so true,
And help each other's faltering steps,
As together we will find
What we are looking for;
Alone we will fail.

Love

Love is magic, sweet and stirring,
Love is togetherness, so endearing;
Keep it alive by always sharing,
Enhance your lives by always caring;
It is not possible to show too much love,
For this is an act created by God above.
Always smile when you meet,
Manifest your love, tender, passionate, and sweet;
Your love, your trust, your comradeship,
Your joys and pleasures too,
Will make every hour, a blessed hour.
Every day a special day, for both of you.

Written in honor of a sister and brother's
15th Wedding Anniversary.

Mr. and Mrs. Ray Carmody
Mr. and Mrs. Vincent Huls

*A Message From Heaven, is an anniversary poem
written for a couple on their Silver Anniversary. They had
one son who was a total invalid from birth and passed away
at the age of 21 years.*

*It tells the story about this young man who gained heaven
through his shining example of endurance. How he
found his young cousin, Carol, in heaven and how they
together with the angels sent a message to his parents
on earth.*

*This message portrays the idea that when one gains heaven,
everyone is alike. That by being there he had total
happiness and could now see, hear, speak, and sing as
everyone else did.*

*He sent this message to his parents on their special day
wishing them love and telling them of this new happiness.*

A Message From Heaven

Twenty-five years together,
Twenty-five years you have shared,
All these years together
With someone who really cared.

God gave you this time together
With your ever-loving spouse,
Your kindness to each other
Made love grow in your house.

Now hear those bells in heaven
Oh! listen to them ring,
Do you hear the music?
Oh! how your heart must sing.

If you listen very carefully
A solo you will hear,
Yes, it is a message from heaven
Sung very loud and clear.

"Congratulations Mom and Dad, I love you,
I am waiting for you here."

*Now the chorus is with the angels
Then a duet we do hear,
As Carol joins in the message
To send our love from here.*

*Be sad only for a moment
Then let your hearts be glad,
We are living with the angels
And are happy Mother and Dad.*

*Now spend your future years together
With an abundance of love and more,
We pray for your eternal happiness
Till the heavens open their doors.*

*Now the duet is finished,
And the chorus has begun,
Keep that love light shining
Till you join up with your son.*

*This is a once in a lifetime occasion
As twenty-five years you have shared,
Twenty-five years together
With everyone who cares.*

Happy Anniversary

A rose with its beauty signifies life,
The thorns the hardships, the stem the strife.
The petals in all glory at the top of the stem
Is the love that has grown from all of them.
As a rose grows more beautiful, so does your life,
When you share your happiness as man and wife;
Happy Anniversary, as with your family you share
Many more years of togetherness, for this wonderful pair.

Love

Love is wealth of riches
That grows with passing years,
It is fragrance of springtime
Cherished are laughter and tears,
Happiness grows with love,
Love nourishes life,
May God bless time shared
As husband and wife.

In honor of my sister and her husband
Mr. & Mrs. Leo Gaspar,
On their 25th Wedding Anniversary.

*A dream **I have dreamed for all of my children** is that they know happiness and their lives be filled with love and laughter. This is not a gift I can give to them, it is something they must cultivate. Each day of their lives can be special if they make it that way.*

Have Love And Life And Laughter

*So . . . don't ever let hate come into your lives . . .
It robs you of health and laughter,
It will drain you of happiness now
And take away love hereafter.
It digs its claws into everything you do,
It will rob you, cheat you, crush you,
Don't ever let hate come into your life
There is nothing more terrible, it is true.
Lift your eyes to God, He will let the light shine through,
Ask Him to help you forgive and forget,
Then there will be love and happiness now and forever,
Don't let hate come into your lives
Have a life full of love and laughter.
For love, is magic sweet and stirring,
Love is togetherness so endearing,
Keep it alive by always sharing
Enhance your lives by always caring,
It is not possible to show too much love
For this is an act created by God above.
Always smile when you meet
Manifest your love, tender, passionate, and sweet,
Your love, your trust, your comradeship,
Your joys and pleasures too,
Will make every hour a blessed hour,
Every day a special day for all of you.
Have Love in your Life and Laughter.*

    *God bless you Vikki and Charlie
    May you know happiness.*

To Be Wanted

Dear little robin, shivering and cold,
Why are you still here, where the north wind blows?
Have your friends left you, will they come when you call?
Come live with me and we will have a ball,
I will make you happy and keep you fat,
We will eat ice cream, cookies, and things like that;
You don't think you would like this very much?
You're leaving tomorrow but will keep in touch?
I am glad to hear this, for the winter is long,
I could not pass the time without your song;
I need to be remembered, just like you,
We need to be with loved ones, who love us so true;
For love is the essence, that makes up the day,
Love is peace, I feel as I pray,
Love is charm, that makes our hearts sing,
Love is a many splendored thing.
See you next Spring!

Untitled

No one ever reached out.
If we'd comfort the lonely
And reach out a helping hand
If we'd help those who need us
There would be love
Throughout the land.

Merry Christmas, To My Family

When you awake this morn
You'll find beneath the tree,
MY HEART,
Filled with Love for thee.
Every beat of my heart,
Every breath I take,
Every thought in my head,
Every movement I do.
Is my Love for you.
May your eyes glow with happiness,
May your heart be filled with joy,
May you show compassion in the things you do.
This is what I want,
This is what I expect of you.

Mother

Life

Learn To Live

Be young while you're young,
Be old when you're old,
This is the way life unfolds.
Live while you're young
To stay alive when you're old,
Your memories will be happy ones
As the days unfold
Be gay and even a little bold,
This relieves your tensions
This I am told.
So learn to live.

Look To This Day

The sky is awfully dark today
Mixed with blue, mixed with gray,
The trees are swaying and bending low
To protect themselves from the winter snow,
It sounds noisy with the distant din
And seems so cold with the winter wind,
But all the darkness will go away
The sun will come out as if to say,
I will change the gray to a charming blue
As I let my warming rays shine through,
I will lighten your heart and quiet your strife,
Look to this day, as it is Life.

Would There Be A Fountain

There should be a fountain
In every city park,
To delight the eyes of children
And cheer a visitor's heart;
It would lull us with watery music
A melody of gurgling and splashing sound,
Rising in a silvery column
And falling back to the ground;
Would there be a fountain
In every public square,
There would be peace and pleasure
For those who visited there.

Silence

Silence is a quiet time
When one can meditate,
Time to think and clear one's thoughts
And time to contemplate.
Silence is a golden word
That brings a motto to mind,
If you don't have something worthy to say
Be silent, at the right time.

A Humorous Deduction

Does one ever reach maturity
That when they are left behind,
They keep their poise and cheerfulness
And are always generous and kind,
And when they are all alone
They keep their peace of mind?

Now the boss is going fishing
In a green and picturesque park,
Or maybe he is taking a trip,
And won't be home till after dark;
Or is it time for his vacation
And you will again be apart?

I think it takes a special kind of person
Who really, really knows,
That her husband doesn't forget her
No matter where he goes;
And on his return from his trips
He will bring her finery and clothes.

I think that they must have spent
Their many years together,
Building this special kind of life;
And when the boss planned his trip,
He must have planned one for his Wife!!

Your Graduation Day

Youth is the richness that you possess today,
Do not waste it as you go along life's way.
There are many hard roads to travel,
With furrows buried deep.
Spend it very carefully and treasures you will reap.
Time passes so swiftly by, do not awaken someday and cry,
"I've done nothing for the world, no, not I."
Be one who in their golden age they still possess,
The riches of their youth, they've known success.
For life is what you make of it,
As up the ladder you climb.
Success is moving forward with the passing of time.

Passing Of Time

An anniversary is the passing of time,
Commemorating a special date,
Of your love and mine.

40th Class Reunion

*Forty years how can it be—
Forty years for you and me.
But if we are honest
We can see
It has been 40 years
For you and me.*

Dear Chum

*Let's visit awhile
Together we will reminisce
Together we will smile.*

Untitled

*It is fun to be wanted,
It is fun to be busy,
But sometimes the speed
Makes me a little dizzy.*

Dearest

The devil no longer controls me.
I made promises to God when I was ill,
But my promises were but a dot of sand
That was whisked away with the first gentle breeze.
Facing surgery didn't stop me,
Nothing did.
The devil kept his ever vigil
And I played and danced with him.
Learned his language,
In fact I got top grades,
I'm his very best student,
But I have a big surprise for him.
When he tries to touch my soul from now on,
I am enrolling in a school of my choice.
One of self-improvement, love, faith, and caring.
And most of all I look forward to tomorrow
When I can put my new learning to good use.
Sharing with you the part of me that involved my past
And the faith of our love that will envelope our future.

Life Is A Gift

*I thought that spring would never come.
The earth, gloomy with sickness and cold,
Had crept into the depth of my soul.
The despair had drained my heart of life's power.
I no longer felt living warmth,
No longer loved life itself.*

*Then warmth appeared, like a breath of sunshine.
It began slowly bringing my soul to life,
Warming the surface of my cold, brittle heart.
I shall never forget my mental despair
As it will help me to remember life is a beautiful gift.*

Be Aware

*I can hear the snowbanks sinking
On this bright and glorious day,
The water seems to be rushing
To hurry winter on its way.*

*The sounds of spring are beautiful
The warmth of the day is great,
Birds in the treetops are singing
The gift of life is great.*

*Don't miss the sound of seasons
It indicates the passing of time,
If you rush through life without stopping
You'll miss all the beauty
That gives you peace of mind.*

Devotion To Yourself

Selfishness is an inner thing,
How much happiness does this act bring?
You get what you want as you take so much,
There is greed in your every touch;
When will you learn it is fun to give,
That giving brings happiness while you live?

Misjudge

How many times have you misjudged someone near and dear,
Because of something you have thought or something you did hear?

Yearning

O! beautiful dream, what happened to you?
I dreamed of life, joyful and new,
A change of old life left behind,
Of a husband so strong, children so kind.
O! beautiful dream, what happened to you?
Is this all mine?
Do I have all I dreamed for?
Am I so blind?
O! beautiful dream, please come true.

Untitled

Don't worry about yesterday for it is gone.

Don't worry about tomorrow
It belongs to God and if He wishes.

Live for today and rejoice.

Untitled

And I shout, I'm an Indian brave and true
And I shout, I'm a warrior
I like to fight, that's not true
I'm just like you.
My skin is a different color,
And I shout, I am a human
I'm just like you, I have feelings too.
When I'm happy, I smile
When sad, I cry
My heart is crushed when a loved one dies.

Heartfelt

My heart stands still
When I hear a cry,
When I hear a cry of pain.

Think What You Miss

If you do not like poetry, think what you miss
Stories told by the fire, long gone by,
The green lighted glowworm and the brilliant firefly;
The memories and dreams of the golden days,
Cut off from the fellowship of great men passed away;
Fairyland, elves, and imaginary things,
The graceful beauty of butterfly wings;
The singing and joy that enters one's heart,
When they hear the melancholy call of the meadowlark;
You miss the lonely cry of the distant train,
As it wails in the night on the vast, quiet plain;
Instead of beautiful gold, crimson, and red,
You notice leaves piled up to rake instead;
You see man without his halo,
And the world without glory,
Disenchantment sums up your lifelong story.

Faucet Drip

Drip drip, drip, drip, drop,
Drip, drip, drop, drip, drop,
Drip Drip Drop;
If my husband doesn't fix it
I will drown before it stops.

Unhappiness

You're not a happy person
What can we do,
Why are you so unhappy
Why are you so blue?

Is life so unbearable
That you must complain,
Can't you be happy
Where lies the blame?

Aren't we considerate?
Aren't we kind?
Maybe we are the cause
Are we so blind?

Don't you know we love you?
Don't you know we care?
Lift your eyes to heaven
Love is everywhere.

*We will try a little harder
And you do the same,
Then we will all know happiness
With no one to blame.*

*Life is not all burdens
Life is not all cares,
Life is full of sunshine
For those who learn to share.*

*Life will be a treasure
When we learn to share,
The burdens of the day
And turn our thoughts to prayer.*

*You're not a happy person
What can we do,
To make you a happy person
We love you so true.*

Lost Love

Others walk together hand in hand,
We are alone in this distant land,
Each to his own, day by day,
Unable to touch, unable to say,
We have lost the way.

When one is lost, how can you go back,
To start over, retrace your tracks?
Do you let time pass you by and by,
Is it worth just one more try?
We have lost the way.

Sometime, somewhere, in days of past,
There was something worthwhile, it didn't last;
Tears turned to dust, hearts turned cold,
No longer the love of days of old,
We have lost the way.

Come O Heavenly One, bring peace,
Let the torment cease;
For hearts that long for strength, security, companionship,
Let them solve their problems, let them find love,
Let them join hands.

Resolutions

*Good-bye '67 Hello '68
I'll make my resolutions
Before I'm too late.*

*Now let me see
Before '68 has begun,
I'll resolve to get up
With the rising sun.*

*I'll do my work gaily
I'll never complain,
I'll do things right
Then I'll not be to blame.*

*I'll brush my teeth
Morning, noon, and night,
To keep my smile
Beautiful and bright.*

*I'll be friendly to all
Cheerful and gay,
I'll spread my love
Throughout the day.*

*I'll fight for my ideals
And do what I can,
To keep America beautiful.*

Nature

Stop A Moment

Wouldn't it be wonderful
To watch each tiny flower,
Open its petals gently
As we wile away the hours?

I think if we would take the time
And take a good long look,
At mother nature's beautiful things
We would fill our memory book.

This little book could mean so much
And Oh! I wonder why,
We rush about our daily chores
And let this beauty pass us by.

Each little leaf could bring a smile
Each flower could enchant you while you look,
There is gracious beauty in the big blue sky
And beauty in the trickling brook.

If you can not spare the time
From your daily chores,
Stop a moment and take a look
All this beauty is yours.

A Value To You

Build yourself a shelterbelt
Enrich your land today,
Five or six rows of trees and bushes
Would be enough I'd say.

It will build up your precious soil
And hold the moisture too,
It has value for your land
Than any other project, you could do.

Plant the bushes closely
So there are no holes to see,
This will provide winter protection
For the pheasant in the tree.

It provides cover, breeding, and nesting
For our wildlife friends,
They provide many hours of enjoyment
From sunrise 'til the day ends.

All of this enjoyment
Recreation, bird-watching, and hunting too,
Would be a rewarding project
For your neighbors and for you.

A New Day Is Born

The sun arose this very morn
And shined on the lake,
A warm, bright orange,
Its beauty reflected
A new day is born.

The day is delightful
The sun is bright,
The brilliance woke us up
From the slumber of night.

With warmth and glory
The land it adorned,
Yes, today as always
A new day is born.

Did You Know

If you do not awaken
    In the deep of the night,
You miss all the beauty
    Of the stars and moonlight,
It is beauty renown,
    An unknown quality
Of silence and sound.

A Quiet Night

The awesome beauty of a quiet night
Are branches of trees in bright moonlight,
Clouds in the sky that float gently by
Melody of mothers as they sing their lullaby,
The croak of the frog along the creek
Gentleness of a lover as he kisses her cheek,
Thoughts in your heart as you see this sight
There is a special beauty in a quiet night.

Listen

Listen to the wind blow
Whistling through the trees,
When it gains momentum
It is no gentle breeze,
The storm clouds gather
The sky turns a deep, dark gray,
Listen to the wind blow
Its warning seems to say,
Find yourself a shelter,
I am the ruler of this day!

Sky Watch With Me At Midnight

I would dislike to be a sound sleeper
Who never awakens at night,
And miss the wealth of riches
That make the sky so bright.

A million stars like fireflies
Twinkle across the sky,
They make a path called the Milky Way
A midnight dream for you and I.

The moon in its highest tower
Makes shadows on the earth below,
As the night rests quiet around us
I hope you too, are watching this moon that glows.

As the astrologer foretells the future
I too shall give it a try,
You will experience immeasurable pleasure
If you awaken to see the heavenly bodies in the sky.

First Day Of Spring '62

As I awoke this morning
A blanket of snow was upon the ground,
Its beauty, its serenity, everywhere could be found;
As I lifted my eyes to heaven
I knew God had been around.
It all started yesterday, the day before spring,
God sent us rain that washed off everything.
The day was warm and glorious, and it cooled later on,
The icicles began to form and the snow started coming down.
Yes, coming down from heaven, to make this wondrous scene,
One only had to open your eyes to know it was no dream.
The trees wore crystal necklaces
The world a bowl of whipped cream,
Look around you, yes, look around my friend,
There is beauty all around you, as seasons begin and end,
It's in your home and children, it's in your job my friend.
All of this was given us, by the wonderful hand of God,
Remember all this glory, but do not linger on,
'Cause as you awoke this morning, springtime has begun.
O! Thank you God, for wintertime, springtime, and sun,
O! Thank you, thank you, thank you, thanks from everyone.

Nature Is A Beautiful Thing

April 19 and the snow came down,
Not just flakes but it fell in mounds,
It covered the grass and it covered the trees,
Within minutes it covered everything you could see,
There was no wind, so it came gently down
It settled softly on the ground;
As it nestled there it was an exciting sight.
Nature is a beautiful thing
It can make you dance, it can make you sing,
Yes, April 19 the snow came down
The flakes were so large they fell in mounds.

First Robin Of Spring

My first robin flitted to a tree,
The first robin of spring, it startled me;
Maybe others have seen it first,
But it made me so happy I thought my heart would burst
A robin is as beautiful as a tree
Its beauty will be enjoyed through all eternity.

The Way It Should Be

You always see two robins
They never seem alone,
When one of them is missing
The other is on the throne.

This is the way it should be
In every form of life,
As two creatures of God together
Form a sacred married life.

Two beautiful robin redbreasts
Both perched in a tree,
Looking at each other
Planning a feathered family.

They make their home together
With mother upon her throne,
Made by the loving work of father
Who picked her for his own.

In this little throne she lays her eggs
Her tiny eggs of blue,
Soon there will be a family
Joining this ever-loving two.

*Have you ever watched the robins
Feed their little family?
Under the watchful eyes of father
They chirp so merrily.*

*They face the world together
And teach their children to fly,
They planned this wonderful occasion
Performed before their eyes.*

*These two robin redbreasts
Seem never to be alone,
They hop, fly, and chirp together
The treetop is their happy home.*

*This is the way it should be
In every form of life,
As two creatures of God together
Form a happy married life.*

A Robin

A robin chirps so merrily,
It is not a quiet bird;
He sings his message clearly,
As he wants it to be heard.

He really has a purpose,
As he flies about the sky;
He sings a tune as he does his work,
So should you and I.

So if together we sing a tune,
He sings his and I sing mine;
Then we know we can lighten your work,
With his chirp and my rhyme.

Spring To Summer

The buds burst out on trees anew,
Spread their leaves against skies so blue.
Grass turns green and flowers bloom,
The birds start singing all in tune,
Days grow long with sun so warm,
Bees join forces and busily swarm,
Children are relieved of school books,
The fish are spawning in the brook,
All these things you will see
As spring changes to summer, for you and me.
Do you know there are people who miss
The change of the season like this?

Come With Me It's Summertime

As I went out to walk this morn
Summer caught me by surprise,
There was no pause between the season
It changed before my eyes.

We shall walk today through the countryside
Along the field and stream,
We'll smell the clover white and pink
And together we will dream.

I've come now to the riverbank
Where the fish glide swiftly by,
There's a twinkly sound as they swim about
Their gracefulness makes me sigh.

To know the grandeur of out-of-doors
The farm is the place to be,
These fertile acres of beloved land
Know boundless beauty, peace, and serenity.

Summer is here to be with us
Take a glimpse of summertime with me,
Enjoy the nature we live close to
And so often never see.

In Whom We Trust

The rain clouds gathered
In the sullen sky,
The rain came down
On land that was dry.

It drank up the water
Like a little sieve,
And burst to green
It had much to give.

This rain gave us flowers
And trickling streams,
The land became beautiful
To enhance our dreams.

As the land is fed
So are all of us,
By the hand of God
In Whom we trust.

Walk With Me In Autumn

*For those who stay within their homes
And do not walk outside,
You miss the personal pleasure
That would fill your heart with pride.*

*I will saunter down the street for you
And tell you what I see,
Now just behind the neighbor's house
Is a scene for you and me.*

*The chrysanthemums are all in bloom
Beneath a crimson tree;
There are squirrels scampering all around
As busy, as busy can be.*

*Now I hear a wonderful sound
Of children playing in the leaves,
I can see their happy smiles
You would enjoy this too, I do believe.*

*As I wander further on
There is an autumn hush,
It murmurs softly in my ears
Take your time, don't rush.*

*I could walk for many a mile
And tell you what I see,
But for you to know the feeling I feel
Step out and walk with me.*

Make Up Of Fall

School bells ring,
    Friendships in swing,
        Children sing.
Bright colored trees,
    Rustle of leaves,
        A cool breeze.
Teacher's meetings,
    Alumni greetings,
        Football beatings.
Homecoming queens,
    Fulfilled dreams,
        Autumn scenes.
Pumpkins orange,
    Harvested corn,
        Squash and acorn.
Goblin's faces,
    Soapy traces,
        Haunted places.
Season changes,
    Farmer's granges,
        Hunting ranges.
Frosted windows,
    Crusty wind blows,
        Restless crows.

Sharing

The children stood beneath the tree
And watched the squirrel eat,
For he had snatched the apple up
That had fallen at their feet.

He scampered up onto a branch
And nibbled anxiously,
The children really didn't mind
They were as happy as they could be.

For sharing is a quality
That some have never known,
And sharing with this animal
Gave pleasure of its own.

A Tree

What do you see when you look at a tree?
Do you see branches gracefully swept
Opening arms neatly kept,
Each season brings changes
In the spring, summer, winter, or fall,
A tree stands stately and it stands tall;
In winter it is undressed, this beautiful tree,
All undressed for the world to see,
Then it is covered with ice and snow
Which makes it twinkle in the moonlit glow,
Spring covers it with little buds
That leap to life in the summer sun,
On these branches gracefully swept
Buds form leaves neatly kept,
Green leaves make shade from the summer sun
Then turn to gold when summer is done,
Take your time and really see
The beautiful mystery of a tree.

His Will Be Done

*Oh, wind! why did you come
And take the leaves away?
I had planned to see their beauty
For many and many a day.*

*You shook them so angrily
I cried for you to stop!
You robbed them of their beauty
On the bottom and the top.*

*Now I suppose you are happy
That you bared them limb for limb,
But I will see their beauty in the springtime
If God wills me to live.*

Untitled

*A new moon off in the distance
Tells us of its mightiness
Large and orange in its hazy distance
Looming above the treetops
Above our homes
Sending romantic images
And chills up and down our spine.*

Cold Winter Sky

The clouds tonight make a fluffy blanket
Against the sky, deep blue,
You will find a beautiful patchwork design
As the moon and the stars burst through.

The moon is outlined by ghostly white
Then pink and shades of blue,
You can feel the warmth in this blanket tonight
As into dreamland it drifts above you.

This Picture You Painted For Me

O Jack Frost, what did you see
As you painted our window tonight,
Did the beauty of our children asleep
Take away your breath on sight?
I know the way you painted so magnificently,
You must have seen a wondrous thing
To paint this picture for me!

The Frosty Ol' Man Of Winter

*I stood one night at my window sill
I could not see outside,
The window was painted so beautiful
It glittered before my eyes.*

*I have been told of a painter
Who has painted for many years,
He dips his brush in buckets of love
And glistens it with his tears.*

*He paints with this depth of feeling
For he can see inside,
Where a whole lifetime unfolds
No wonder he paints with pride.*

*For eight little children have entered this home
A family of ten, within reside,
And year after year he does his work
From his frosty perch outside.*

Winter Plea

*Please don't bend O majestic tree
And break before my eyes,
You crinkle and crackle like a piece of glass
Oh! why?   Oh! why?   Oh! why?*

*Did the rain that came gently down
Turn icy and cling to you?
You look like a giant crystal
You do,   you do,   you do.*

*If the wind came swiftly along
To bend your trunk, I'd certainly try,
Like the boy and the dike, I'd hold you up
Say I,   say I,   say I.*

*Please don't bend O majestic tree
And break before my eyes,
For if you would lay your beauty down
I'd cry,   I'd cry,   I'd cry.*

*Oh! do be gentle Mr. Wind
Be careful of my tree,
Its beauty is here for all of us
To see,   to see,   to see.*

*O God, You must be standing there
Smiling down on me,
Because I worry oh! so much, about
A tree,   a tree,   a tree.*

Friendship

Is This You

*If you look into your mirror
And can see what you have done,
To bring happiness to others
Then your soul has won.*

*If there is a smile on your heart
From memories of friendships true,
Friendships built on trust and generosities,
Then you can be proud this image is you.*

*If there is laughter in your voice
As you meet the trials each day,
Then you will add happiness
To many along the way.*

*Happiness comes from what you do for others
No matter how small it may be,
It is your thoughtfulness from within
That makes you beautiful to see.*

*If you look within yourself
And this image is what you see,
Then you have succeeded
And will rejoice eternally.*

Memories

If only I were a painter
I would paint this precious scene,
One we will always remember
Even in our dreams.

It was our last visit
With the dearest of old friends,
He was our friend and neighbor
His given name was Ben.

We took our children with us
To bid our last good-bye,
At that time we didn't know it
But soon he was to die.

As we left him that evening
We looked back at him from afar,
The sun shone on his aged head
We wanted to turn back the car.

*He was standing between two stately trees
With his resting bench near by,
He looked so bent and aged
It made us want to cry.*

*He's resting now in heaven
Rewarded for his kind deeds,
We will always treasure our memories
As I cannot paint this scene.*

*A silhouette of Ben
Against the setting sun,
A picture of a man
With his lifetime work well done.*

*How many of you remember
As you read this heartfelt poem,
Of someone dear in your life
Who leaves memories that enchant your home?*

My Blind Friend

For one who cannot see the wonder
Of this autumn scene,
Let my eyes be your eyes
And paint for you a dream.

Can you picture a giant
With arms and fingers spread,
Dressed all in autumn splendor
Of golds and oranges and red?

The splendid robes upon him
Began a deep dark green,
But the warmth and glory from heaven
Gave us this autumn scene.

May my lips speak of the beauty
And fill your longing heart,
With pictures of true splendor
That keep you and the world apart.

The spring flowers now are fading
But there still are some in bloom,
Even though they are passing
There is no intended gloom.

As the earth will regain its splendor
You will regain your sight,
Because God is waiting in heaven
To give you what is right.

You have earned this glory
And your happiness will be foretold,
On the clouds and stars above us
As your eternal life unfolds.

My Crippled Friend

*As I climb the mountain for you
And my breath is coming hard,
I understand the hurdle you face
As you cross your own front yard.*

*The cliff is becoming steeper
With many a scraggly rock . . .
Now I take the time to wonder
How you ever walked a block.*

*The mountain now seems insurmountable
And the temperature will drop,
But there will be rejoicing in heaven
When together we reach the top.*

Untitled

*You're a very special person
This I have found is true
You're energetic, organized, composed,
Compassionate, and fair.
You're a friend, you show you care.
This is Pam, this is you.*

*Even though we are unable to bring sound to our deaf friends,
we can tell them of beautiful things that only hearing
people are aware of, if we learn to speak their language.
This is a poem I wrote many years ago for my daughter, who is
hard of hearing, and her friends.*

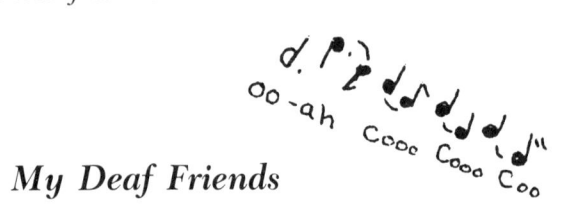

My Deaf Friends

*I have learned your language,
And even though I try,
My fingers cannot tell you of a tiny baby's cry.
Of the thump of the shoes as the baby crawls,
The chimes of the clock that hangs on the wall,
Clap of hands of children in fun,
Clatter of hoofs as the horses run.
The strain of music from the concert in the park,
Or roar of the plane in the sky after dark.
The crack of lightning and the patter of rain,
The gurgle of water as it disappears down the drain,
Rumble of thunder in the heavens above,
The oo-ah cooo cooo coo, of the turtle dove.
May you know the feeling, the urge I feel for life
My friends who cannot hear,
For you have given much to me,
And may God give me the time,
To spell my love out to you, on these fingertips of mine.*

Does Anyone Hear Me?

*I am deaf. I want to scream.
I want someone to hear me,
But if I scream how will I know
Anyone heard me?
I cannot even hear myself.
My deaf friends are not here
And I need someone to talk to.*

*I see someone over there,
She seems friendly.
I will tell her I need someone
To talk to, I'll sign.
My fingers are racing frantically,
She is smiling,
Oh God let her understand!
She shrugged her shoulders.
She is walking away.*

*My world is so small
And I am all alone.*

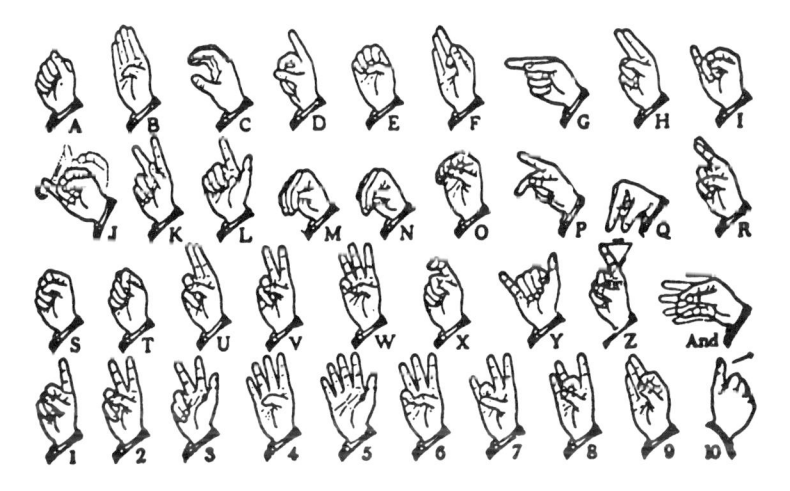

Let Me See So That I May Hear

Spring, that special time for growth.
The season that makes you aware, it electrifies your senses.
You watch for each blade of grass, listen for the first song bird.
How beautiful! Do we take the time to think of those who cannot appreciate all the beauty because they are handicapped?
Are We Aware!

I am writing of deaf awareness, Deaf Awareness is recognized in May, Are we aware for only one week, do we understand or even care?

I have a dream, a dream that sign-language become a universal language. That sign-language be taught in every school, starting with the sign of love, in kindergarten and continued until it is as common as the English language. This would eliminate one handicap and close the communication gap forever.

Can you imagine the impact if the elderly who lost their hearing would no longer sit in silence, the injured, sick, hearing impaired and even the people without handicaps could communicate with no barriers. We can go to the moon, but we cannot talk to a deaf neighbor!

The deaf can see to hear, we can see and hear but cannot speak! If there is an educator, a legislator or anyone who can make the dream come true, stand up and be counted. Let us not turn away. Let's reach out and touch each other, let's use our fingers so they may see and hear.
We Care!

NFO's Troublesome Days

What has happened to the old hometown?
Why the sadness, why the frowns?
Did they stop to think what their actions might do?
Will this action help all of you?
God gave this rich land to all of us
Let us stay neighbors and friends,
This way we will grow strong with trust
There will be just a beginning, no end.

Why Poetry

Poetry charms a ladies heart . . .
Puts a smile on your face
Sends chills down your spine
And brings tears to one's eyes.

Telling It Like It Is

When I awoke this morning I thought it would be lots of fun,
To do a little shopping before I got my housework done.
So, I dressed up in my finery put makeup on my face,
Glanced at my clock, and hurried from my place.
Jumped into my car and sped away so fast,
For I really had to hurry or the sales would never last.
I found myself a parking place, and rushed into the store.
I looked for many items, through twenty aisles or more
I found my husband's shaving needs, his deodorant, and his soap,
Now the crowd was getting bigger, and I really had to cope
I checked off my list, which was really very long,
For the store had promised me, I would get it for a song.
I needed toothpaste, hand cream, blush, mascara, and things like that.
I also needed lipstick, to match my new hat.
Now I looked in many aisles, and the toothpaste was on sale,
Right there was a rain check, I missed it, "Oh! What the _____!"
I needed a gift for Mother, a friend, and baby Sue.
I went from counter to counter, I didn't know what to do.
By then my feet were hurting and the time was flying fast,
I grabbed something from the shelf as I was hurrying past.
I went to the checkout, and waited patiently in line.
The lady ahead of me needed a price check, it happens all the time.
By then I was exhausted and tried not to be irate,
For I had glanced at my clock, and was really running late.

I finally made my purchase, went home, hung up my hat and coat.
I was tired and hungry, and had missed my favorite soap.
I had just pulled myself together, when the AVON lady came.
She comes in any weather
I opened the door, and didn't give her a chance,
I said "NO," but was met with a friendly glance.
She said, "I would like to help you save money, energy, gas, and time,"
By bringing her store to my door, I would even save a dime.
She said," I have an unconditional guarantee,
That if I was not happy with my purchase,
She would exchange or refund for me."
She said, "I will leave my lovely samples and I could give them a try."
For if I got to know her product, I would surely want to buy.
She could see that I was busy, so she left her ACB.
That stands for AVON CALLING BACK, she would keep in touch with me.
She made her next appointment, showed her demos, and then was on her way.
I even gave her an order, of the things I had forgotten today.
Now I have learned my lesson, and I will tell my friends,
How easy it is to shop AVON, and save money in the end!

        By Rosemarie McCoy
        Your AVON Representative
        GIVE ME A CALL, I WANT YOUR BUSINESS!

Warm Their Hearts This Christmas

*The splendor of autumn
Brings us the chilling cold,
It turns our thoughts to Christmas
As leaves turn crimson and gold.*

*Now I would like to help you
Choose gifts for one and all,
For in our Avon catalogue
We have gifts that are big and small.*

*I'll introduce you to a new fragrance
One that will win his heart,
And I promise he'll remember you
Even when you are apart.*

*The name of this cologne is "TEMPO"
A soft and joyful scent,
For moments that go beyond words
It is money wisely spent.*

*We have sachets in Christmas wrappings
Both powders and oils too,
They are put in lovely decanters
Collector's items to please all of you.*

*We will dress your home in holiday splendor
Beauty will greet your friends,
With candlesticks, cruets, and Christmas gifts
In all the latest trends.*

*We have pomanders for your bathrooms
Toothpaste, hair care, brushes and combs,
We have all your daily needs
And you can buy them in your home.*

*You'll be happy for your children
On this special Christmas day,
When Sweet Pickles Clean-Up Gang
Help you to bring good grooming their way.*

*We have something to catch the fancy
Of all men, young or old,
We have shower soap-on-a-rope
Which makes it easy to hold.*

*And after they step from the shower,
All refreshed and clean,
They can shave and splash on cologne
He is the answer of your dream.*

*What more can I say to convince you
To give Avon a try
As we have the famous guarantee
On everything you buy.*

*So when I ring your doorbell
Open your door up wide,
And let me bring these lovely things
All inside.*

MERRY CHRISTMAS and GOD'S BLESSING
 on YOU during the NEW YEAR.

Rose McCoy, Your Avon Representative

Farewell Fine Friends 'Til We Meet Again

Remember the stories our parents told?
Remember the apples and watermelon we stole?
The tricks we played on Halloween,
Humbolt High and the school scenes,
Buffalo Trading Post, with Don and Si
The oversized ice-cream cones, we did buy.
Wall Lake trips and all the dates
Wedding dances and getting home late,
Remember Marcella, the bloody nose,
That turned out to be a red, red rose?
The old north bus and the cattle truck,
The experiences we lived through with just plain luck;
The steak we ate on Friday night
It was sinful to eat, but it tasted alright.
The parties and picnics that we shared,
The fun we had with friends who cared;
McKennan Hospital and our blessed event
When out on a party our hubbies went,
The hats Pat smashed, and the parties we crashed
The cold night Pat left Mac hunting for his keys
Digging in the snow on his hands and knees,
Pat drove away and out of sight
Neither will admit it, but I think they were tight,
Because neither seemed to know it was 16 below zero that night.
We'll always remember the days gone by,
We really hate to see you go,
As we watched each other's children grow;
We all will miss you very much
But through our letters we will keep in touch,
And when to your new house you go
Have health and happiness, and make lots of dough!

I Am Sorry

If there is someone you have hurt today,
By words, or touch, or sign;
Let them know you are sorry,
Show them you can be kind.

When someone is hurt, and tears do not show,
You can be sure they are crying inside,
So think about what you have done
And say, "I am sorry," it helps to swallow your pride.

Hurt has a way of breaking one's heart,
And builds up a wall so high,
If you are the one who has ever been hurt,
You know what it is like to cry.

Never let a day go by
That you have not stopped and said,
"I am sorry"
Before your pillow touches your head.

If there is someone you have hurt today,
By words, or touch, or sign;
Let them know you are sorry,
Show them you can be kind.

Patriotism

The Passing Of A Great Man

*The death of Martin Luther King
Has proved to the world an important thing
That no matter the creed or color of skin
We all know anguish with the loss of our kin.
Let the passing of this man
Cry out to all lands, "We are created equal."*

*Under the canopy of heaven, we hear him say,
"Don't sing of the praises I have won
But of love, peace, and unity beneath the sun,
Tell the people to open their eyes
Because it is for peace that I died."
For evil must give way for power of good
This was his belief for which he stood.*

*His kindness and love of all mankind
Has left a legacy behind
For his family, friends, and for you and me
May we carry on his work for Freedom and Liberty.*

We Want Peace

The birds awake
One by one,
They sing their message
To the rising sun.

They sing gaily
When they sing at dawn,
They sing all day
'Til day is gone.

As one chirps Good-Morning
The others chirp Hi!
Their message gains volume
When it reaches the sky.

Does it make you wonder
As they sing one by one,
If there is a chain reaction
From sun to sun?

*Does it make you wonder
Of this beautiful song,
Are they joining voices
Miles and miles long?*

*Do they keep singing
This message of glee,
Are their chirps heard
From sea to sea?*

*Could we tell the birds
And they tell their friends,
How we want peace
That will never end.*

*I know this is quite a job
To tell a little bird,
So let us join in prayer
Our message will be heard.*

The Flag Waves We Pray

*I know why the flag waves
On the neighbor's house each day,
I know, and so do they.*

*Three sons lived there once
But are now away,
We know why the flag waves, and so do they.*

*We no longer hear the sounds
Of young men moving 'round,
Nor do they, nor do they.*

*The flag will always wave
If God wills, they will not stay,
He will return them safe someday.*

*As the flag waves
We kneel to pray,
That God wills, they return someday.*

All Alone On Christmas

Christmas this year, I will be all alone
As my son is off to war;
He is fighting for freedom, peace, and love,
As his father did before.
His father died a soldier,
He gave his life for us.
"Why now must my son be fighting,
Why should there be a war,
Why must each generation fight,
For what their fathers did before?"
Because we have a great country;
With freedom and liberty for all,
For this my son is fighting,
For this my son stands tall.
There will always be an America,
A great country for you and for me;
For brave fathers and sons will always fight,
To keep America free.

Cry Die! Not I!

We don't want war, the voices cry,
We will do without, rather than die,
We will do without, if they won't give,
We will do without, so we can live;
We will build our resources and stack them high,
We will work together, we will not die!
We are Americans, proud and strong,
We will find a solution, for war is wrong.
Pain and terror in our hearts,
Anguish and tears, flesh torn apart,
This is the picture of war;
We do not want this, we have tried before.

Wake Up

"Come down from your Ivory Tower"
And face the world of today;
There are more important decisions,
Than little things that get in your way.

"Come down from your Ivory Tower"
Do not withdraw from this world of action and war;
Face up to your responsibilities,
As you have never done before.

"Come down from your Ivory Tower"
And show us what you can do;
To make this world a better place to live in,
With peace and contentment the world through.

Freedom And Liberty

If countries work together
And join hands from sea to sea,
What a wonderful world this would be!

Age old problems are solved,
By understanding and love,
What a wonderful world this would be
If all would know Freedom and Liberty.

Boyhood To Manhood

*The boys in our neighborhood have left us
To fight a war for peace,
May God guide their footsteps
And may their faith increase.*

Christmas Without Them

*How can we celebrate Christmas
With all the boys away?
We will join in a mass meeting
Bend our knees and pray.
Jesus was born on Christmas
To save the world from sin,
The boys are fighting for freedom
To make homes safe for their kin.
We will try to be gay and happy
As the boys would want us to be,
For they are fighting so their loved ones
Will always have a Christmas tree,
For the tree is a symbol of Christmas,
Love, Freedom, and Liberty.*

The Sun Rained Tears That Day

The sun came up
      in the distant sky,
Clouded over now
      I wonder why?
Did it know seven were coming,
      but soon would die?
It watched the astronauts
      with sadness and love,
And saw it all
      from its perch above.
Seven entered the shuttle
      with eager steps,
And it watched again
      as the people wept.
It was all too sudden
      to understand,
The world was hushed
      throughout the land.
As the sun went down
      it bid good-bye,
Clouded over now
      it could cry.

In remembrance of the Challenger Astronauts
The "Challenger" exploded in flight on
January 28, 1986.

Eight Bailed Out

*Eight bailed out
In the darkness of night,
Eight bailed out
In horror and fright.*

*The motor stopped
The sky became a blaze,
Everything in turmoil
Everyone dazed.*

*They staggered to the door
And tumbled out,
A prayer in their hearts
Their lips gave a shout.*

*Hurry, there's no time
Let me help, my friend,
Together we will make it
Together we will descend.*

*The tumble was fierce
They descended so fast,
The parachutes exploded
As they opened the clasp.*

*A Hand from heaven
Guided them down,
And kept them together
'Til they were found.*

*A tired, hungry group
With a victory scored,
They shared their fright
And much, much more.*

*This little group
Repaired their health,
And went on fighting
For their country's wealth.*

*For "Freedom of Liberty",
For "Freedom of Speech",
Our gift from God
Everyone must reach.*

Searching For Strength

I Am With You

*I am thinking of your loss
That is much the same as mine.
They say the pain will go away
If we just give it time.*

*How can time replace our loss
When our loved one is gone.
We know that death is final
There is no room for song.*

*They did not want to leave us
They only wanted to stay.
But God put out a call
And called them home today.*

*Now we must think of others
Who need our loving touch.
This will remove our pain
And help us very much.*

*By doing things for others
It may help wipe our tears away.
Maybe we can smile again
And face another day.*

*Others too are grieving
And now we understand.
It is time for us
To give a helping hand.*

Their Loss Is Our Loss

The yellow roses swayed gently
    As they adorned his casket brown;
Our thoughts were with his loved ones,
    As they commended his body to the ground.

Father's Day—1989 McKennan Hospital

Father of my children,
Take my hand Mac, and together we will climb
The highest mountain, sing the loudest song,
And sit and watch the birds together.
Together what a beautiful word,
I never knew until now the true meaning.
From this day on we have faith, we have hope—
We will fight for every precious moment together.
We will be together—take my hand I love you.
Together we shall dance our last dance—together.

      Love you
      Rose

You're Special

May God bless you in this time of strife
    And give you the strength to continue life,
Give you the will to face this trial
    Help you again to smile.
God knows and loves you.

True Love

Good morning, good morning, good morning
I love you – you – you.
As the sun arises on the horizon
I pledge my love so true.
Sleepily we snuggle together, together you and I.
We don't need to express ourselves,
For my whole world is complete when you are nearby.

Dad

With minds wide open and arms outstretched
We grasp for hope.
Hope becomes reality when tests return
And God opens little doors
Letting us know He is on our side.
Sleep on my darling, rest your tired heart.
For tomorrow is a new day.

Cel

As days and nights pass swiftly by
And years keep adding on.
The moments spent with you
Are the most precious of all.

Untitled

We asked for one more miracle
And God did hear and see
He heard and sent relief to thee
Just one more miracle,
You've been so good to me.

Going Home

Warm greetings and a handshake
Were always there; he cared.
His spirit was high, he was going home.

A thank you and an appreciative smile
Made you want to linger awhile
His spirit was high, he was going home.

He held me close, quiet times we shared
In those loving moments I knew he cared
His spirit was high, he was going home.

Why did he talk and sing, when I wanted to cry?
He knew why.
His spirit was high, he was going home.

His sons and daughters were always there
They shared; he cared.
His spirit was high, he was going home.

His Faith, Courage, and Wisdom he shared with all.
His spirit was high as he answered God's call.
He was going home.

Mom wrote this poem while dad was in hospice.

Friends In Hospice

Father Murray, Father Flannery, Sisters,
Doctors, nurses, volunteers,
Cleaning, and maintenance.

Mac sang me this little song this morning.
February 23, 1990

Be my protection, by my side
Be my protection, by my side
Be my protection, by my side

And in love and remembrance, I will finish his song
And dedicate it to you.

Be my protector, be my guide
Give me strength, give me pride
Give me dignity, as I die
Give me strength, as I gave as a man
Stand beside me, hold my hand
Be by protection, by my side.

Mac passed away February 25, 1990.

Have You Ever

Have you ever been discouraged, and this is what you said,
"I'm so terribly unhappy, I wish that I were dead."
Then you turn your head around, and what do you see?
You see your happy children, as wonderful as can be.
They are your stairsteps to heaven, given to you and to me.
Gather up your courage and kneel down to pray.
Strengthen your footsteps as you go along the way.
If you stop to count your blessings, this is what you will say.
"Every day can be beautiful, day, after day, after day."

Find Strength In God

I cannot cry
My feelings are too deep,
I must be strong,
Only within do I weep.
Where is the smile
That I must wear?
I must be strong
To show I care.

Unending Love

"Until death us do part",
  Words uttered in softness,
Now remembered in such depth
  It breaks my heart.

A vow of unending love
  That only death could take away.
My soul racks with pain —
  You left me today.

Wretched word death —
  To you a release.
You left sickness and troubles behind,
  You found peace.

Now me — I must cut the ties of yesteryear,
  I must find my way.
Through our never-ending love and faith
  I will find strength today.

Stumble I will through this darkened earth.
    Running — crying — screaming.
I will fall then pick myself up.

I wish for no more loneliness,
    Nightmarish dreams — sleepless nights.

I'm going home to children small
    This will help fill the void —
The empty space — Grandpa's place.

Their hugs and kisses are warm
    They need me now, like I need them
Now, I must go home to a new life
    A grandmother now, instead of a wife.

I won't be alone — they will be near,
    They will fill my life — no more tears.
I can get through today
    And look forward to tomorrow.

Untitled

*I have slipped to deep depths in my anguish,
Missing your touch and your smile.
I felt I lost both you and my Savior,
And I have gripped for a lifeline
As I face each new trial.*

*I need to draw the strength from memories
Of your courage and the good times we shared.
I need to remember the happiness
And look to a bright new day,
For the darkness of despair will be erased.*

*If I only remember to pray,
But answers to prayer are not always visible
And prayers not easily said.
When one has the courage to realize
That you are not really dead.
You will live on my sweetheart, in another world
That keeps you and I physically apart.
A place where you share God's love.*

Untitled

*O God, hear my prayers
See my anguish
Give me strength to lift myself up
And become a positive person.
Let me be a support to my children
And help me to understand
Why You chose to take my loved one.
Stand beside me, hold my hand
And lead me into a brighter future,
For this I pray, Amen.*

Untitled

*Mary, you are here
In the church, in my heart,
And in my home.
Your door was open
When my loved one entered
The kingdom of heaven.
Leave it unlocked so that when
I am called I can enter heaven
Through your door.*

*For you have always been with me,
As a child when I felt pain
Loneliness — when I felt left out
Also in my joyful times — when I baked a cake,
Cleaned the chapel, and as I grew older,
Held my children.*

*And you were there when my dear one died.
You held us close and when he had to leave
You led the way.*

*For we both believed in your love for us.
You will be forever close to my heart,
Even in my darkest hour.*

Life Was Made For Living

*I am thinking of your loss
That is much the same as mine,
They say the pain will go away
If we but give it time.*

*How can time replace our loss
When our loved one is gone.
We know that death is final
There is no room for song.*

*They did not want to leave us
They only wanted to stay,
But God put out a call
And called them home today.*

*Now we must think of others
Who need our loving touch,
This will remove our pain
And help us very much.*

*By doing things for others
It may help to wipe our tears away,
Maybe we can smile again
And face another day.*

*Others too are grieving
And now we understand,
It is time for us
To give a helping hand.*

*For life was made for living
And positive we must be,
If we console others
Our grief will be set free*

*So ask God for courage and strength
For today and tomorrow combined,
For we'll join our loved ones in heaven
If we are only kind.*

Poetry

By

Celestine (Mac) McCoy

Over There

That 20 years have passed
And the U.N. is still aghast.

The world continues to boil
With the victors go the spoils.

How senseless war can be
When will man have tranquility?

Draftees are soberly waiting their call
And wonder if it's worth it all?

Our only salvation must be
To bow our head and bend a knee.

    C. R. McCoy

The Cresting Of A Wave

How often do we wonder at the wonder of a tree
Or of a wave that has a high or low, never in between
Or of a boy or girl, who is a victim of muscular dystrophy
Here is life and its bounty crammed into a score
Man has traveled to the edge of space
The impossible thought before
The chasms of space soon to be explored
Will be no more revealing
Than if T.B. and M.D. were in rapport
There must be a solution or a key
In the prevention and cure of muscular dystrophy.

    Celestine McCoy

Time Lapse

Memories of youth, prime of life, middle age,
The golden years, bring thoughts of why we are here.

Giving, learning to receive, caring, and love, all persevere.

Hate, mistrust, and thoughtless self-interest
Slows the clock of life, to a state of fear.

Oh, if all people on this spaceship earth,
Could expose themselves to the camera of life
Not with disinterest, but with love and cheer.

                Mac

Happy Birthday Loved One

God bless you Love
Protect you my Dear
And keep you happy
Throughout the year.

        Your Loving Husband

My Wife

My wife is still my sweetheart
Though my hair has turned to gray,
We have a mutual understanding
That puts highlights in my day.

She is sweet and tender
There is starlight in her eyes,
She is my constant companion
My friend until I die.

Celestine

Inspirations In Faith

Inspirations 1	Today's Prayer For The Future 5
Let Me Key Your Mind To Mine 2	A Child At Play 6
Creation 2	Little Lost Girl 6
With Us He Will Stay 3	A Little Child Walked 7
Heaven's Answering Service 3	A Prayer For Help 8-9
Serenity 4	Help Me Enter Port 10-11
Farewell 'Til Tomorrow 5	

Family

Mother 15	My Son 31
These Are The Bonds 16-17	Through The Eyes Of A Child 32
Golden Years 18	Growth 33
For You The Bell Rings 19	Children 33
Father 20	Gift From Heaven 34
Please Help Mother Is My Prayer 21	Our Little Star 35
I Will Always Hear The Bells 21	A Little Mixed Up 36
Please Help My Father 21	Happy Birthday Sandy! 36
Dearest On Father's Day 22	Sing Of Lisa 37
Cel 23	Lisa 37
Remember Me With Love 24	Girls 38
Lucky Pop On Father's Day 24	On The Most Wanted List 38
Sculptured By Two 25	Seasons Present A Bit Of Confusion 39
Whatever I Do 26-27	Treasure Chest 40
Precious Moments 28	Mommy's Love Will Help You 41
Place For Baby 28	Tribute To Emil 42
Thought Complete 28	The Church Was Filled With People .. 42
First Born 29	Nettie 43
Happy Birthday To Our Daughter 29	Barney And Glady 44
A Rainy Day 30	Grandmother's Thanks 45
You 30	Ruby Wedding Anniversary 46-49

There are several Untitled poems throughout the book. These reflect poems that mom wrote but had not titled.

Love

Think Of One Word........................53
Love 53
Melody Of Love 53
A Phrase..54
Love Is Happiness 54
Song In Our Hearts 55
Remember Him With Love 55
Today Is Forever 56
Remember......................................57

Love 58
A Message From Heaven 59-61
Happy Anniversary........................62
Love 62
Have Love And Life And Laughter....63
To Be Wanted 64
No One Ever Reached Out..............64
Merry Christmas, To My Family 65

Life

Learn To Live 69
Look To This Day 69
Would There Be A Fountain 70
Silence..70
A Humorous Deduction 71
Your Graduation Day 72
Passing Of Time 72
40th Class Reunion.........................73
Dear Chum 73
It Is Fun To Be Wanted 73
Dearest..74
Life Is A Gift.................................75

Be Aware..75
Devotion To Yourself......................76
Misjudge..76
Yearning...77
Don't Worry About Yesterday...........77
And I Shout, I'm An Indian Brave.....78
Heartfelt...78
Think What You Miss 79
Faucet Drip....................................79
Unhappiness 80-81
Lost Love 82
Resolutions 83

Nature

Stop A Moment 87
A Value To You 88
A New Day Is Born........................89
Did You Know 89
A Quiet Night 90
Listen 90
Sky Watch With Me At Midnight 91
First Day Of Spring '62....................92
Nature Is A Beautiful Thing.............93
First Robin Of Spring 93
The Way It Should Be 94-95
A Robin..96
Spring To Summer 96

Come With Me It's Summertime 97
In Whom We Trust........................98
Walk With Me In Autumn...............99
Make Up Of Fall..........................100
Sharing 101
A Tree 101
His Will Be Done 102
A New Moon...............................102
Cold Winter Sky 103
This Picture You Painted For Me 103
The Frosty Ol' Man Of Winter........104
Winter Plea 105

Friendship

Is This You 109
Memories 110-111
My Blind Friend 112
My Crippled Friend 113
You're A Very Special Person 113
My Deaf Friends 114
Does Anyone Hear Me? 115
Let Me See So That I May Hear 116
NFO's Troublesome Days 117
Why Poetry 117
Telling It Like It Is 118-119
Warm Their Hearts This Christmas . 120-121
Farewell Fine Friends 122
I Am Sorry 123

Patriotism

The Passing Of A Great Man 127
We Want Peace 128-129
The Flag Waves We Pray 130
All Alone On Christmas 131
Cry Die! Not I!, ... 132
Wake Up 133
Freedom And Liberty 133
Boyhood To Manhood 134
Christmas Without Them 134
The Sun Rained Tears That Day 135
Eight Bailed Out 136-137

Searching For Strength

I Am With You 141
Their Loss Is Our Loss 142
Father's Day 1989 142
You're Special 142
True Love 143
Dad 143
Cel 144
We Ask For One More Miracle 144
Going Home 145
Friends In Hospice 146
Have You Ever 147
Find Strength In God 147
Unending Love 148-149
I Have Slipped To Deep Depths 150
O God, Hear My Prayers 150
Mary, You Are Here 151
Life Was Made For Living 152-153

Poetry By Celestine (Mac) McCoy

Over There 157
The Cresting Of A Wave 157
Time Lapse 158
Happy Birthday Loved One 158
My Wife 159